BOOM TO THE MOON

BY STUART GREEN

THIS BOOK IS DEDICATED TO HEIDI,
WHO I HOPE WILL ALWAYS
AIM FOR THE MOON.

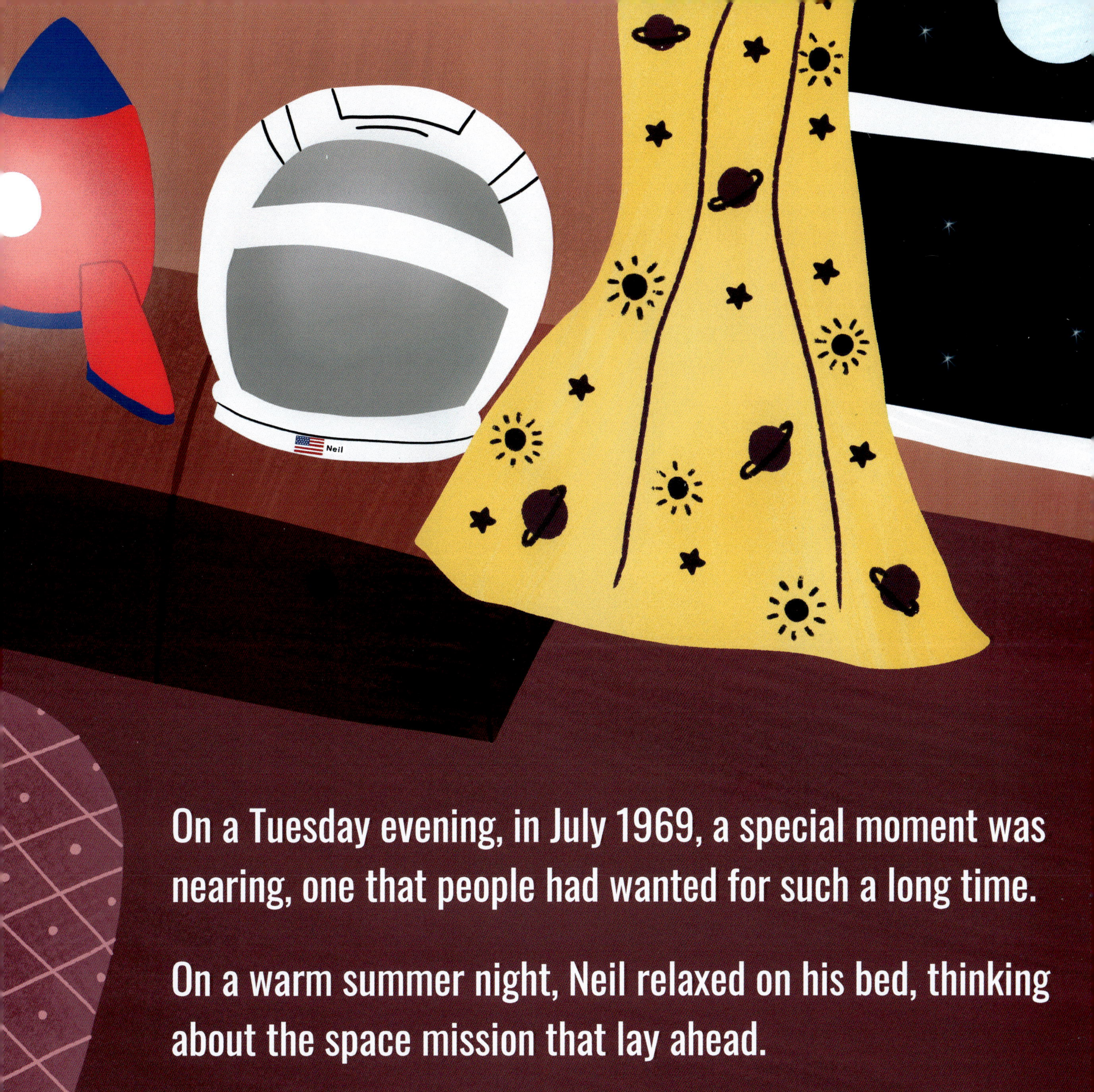

On a Tuesday evening, in July 1969, a special moment was nearing, one that people had wanted for such a long time.

On a warm summer night, Neil relaxed on his bed, thinking about the space mission that lay ahead.

Throughout the night, he dreamt of what would be happening soon; for he knew the next day; he would be flying to the

MOON!

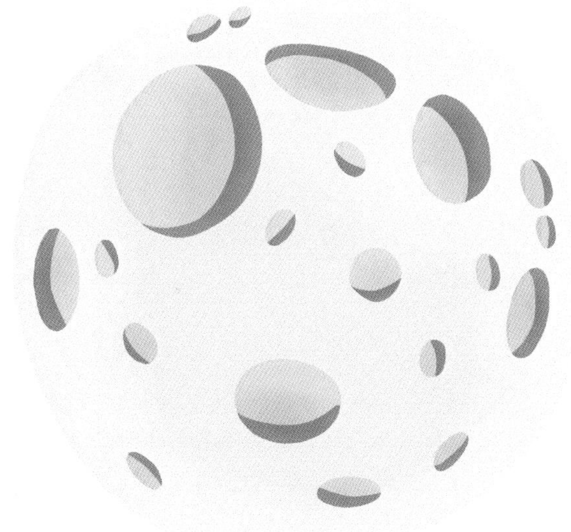

He woke up at 04:00 and jumped out of his bed, with a spring in his step, he ran downstairs and he said...

“I’m flying to the Moon today! The **MOON**!” he said.

I'm flying
to the
Moon
today.

Without a second thought he jumped into his car,
whilst driving he looked up and saw a twinkling star.

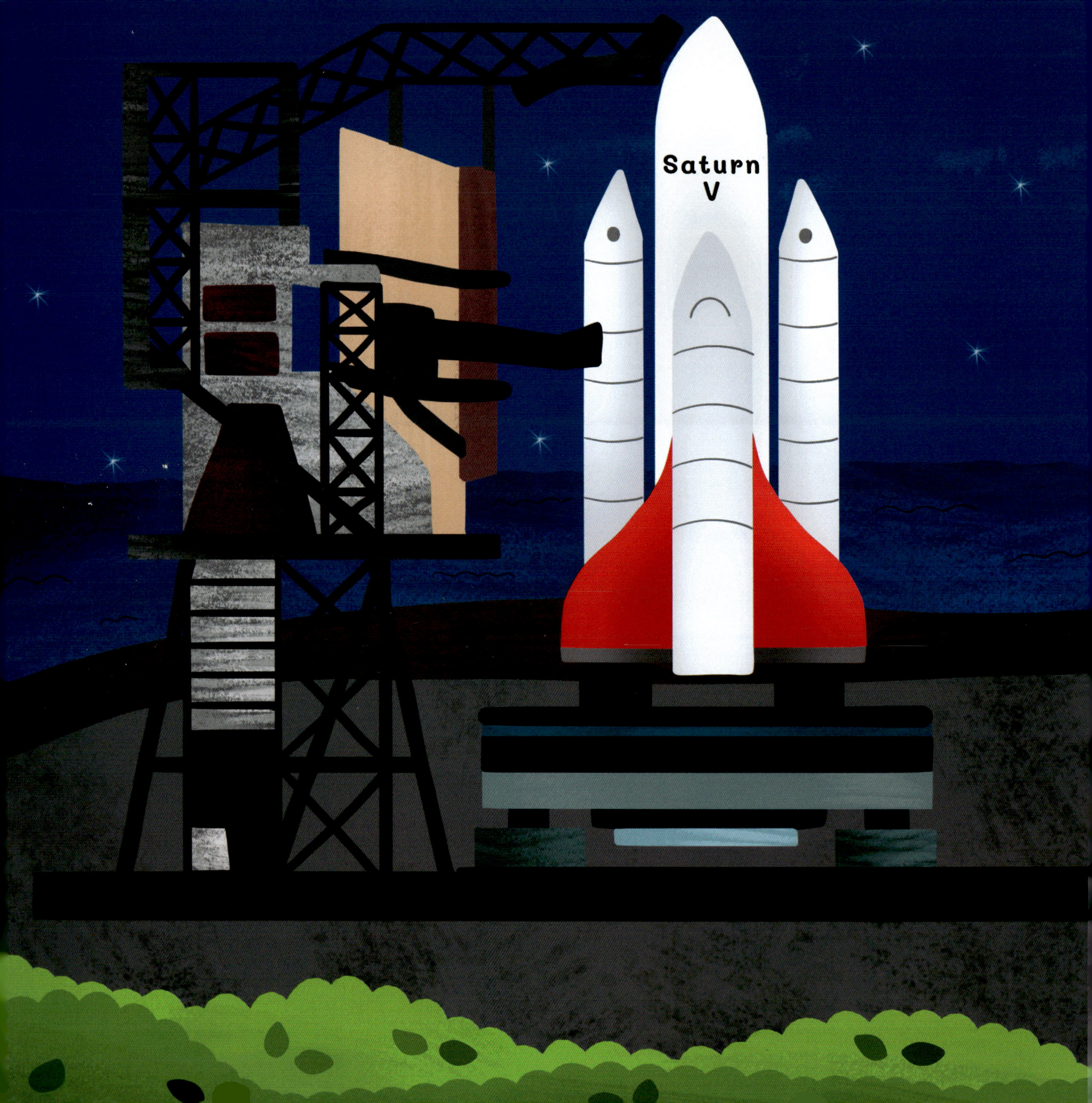
Saturn
V

He parked at the launchpad where the rocket stood tall, and waited patiently for his friend Buzz to give him a call.

A few moments went by until Buzz did eventually call, "I'm on my way Neil, I can hardly wait! We're going to have a ball."

Neil burst with joy as he saw Buzz approaching down the road, a joy so overpowering, he thought he might **EXPLODE**!

The time had arrived to begin the big **ADVENTURE,** both excited to present the world with a glimpse of their **FUTURE**.
Ther
goin
now
Neil
Neil
Apollo

They belted themselves in,
after crawling to their seat,
“there’s no going back now
Buzz, we’re in for a real
TREAT.”
Buzz
Buzz
Apollo

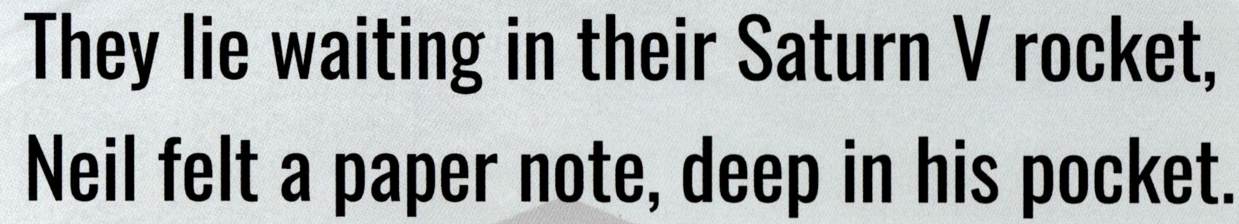

They lie waiting in their Saturn V rocket,
Neil felt a paper note, deep in his pocket.

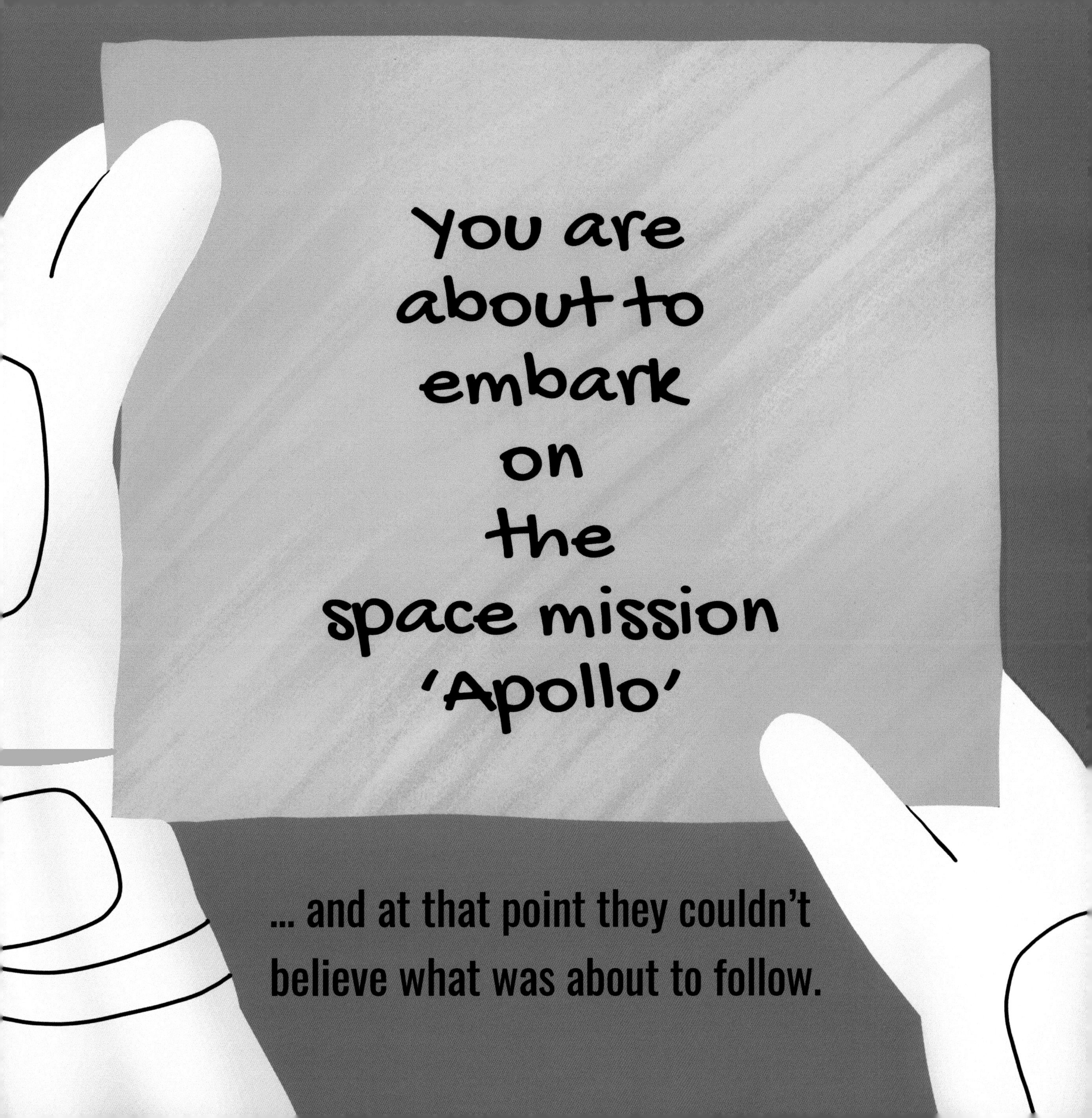

You are
about to
embark
on
the
space mission
'Apollo'

... and at that point they couldn't believe what was about to follow.

With the rocket filled to the brim with fuel,
Neil and Buzz smiled, "THIS IS SO SO COOL!"
This is so so cool
Neil
Apollo
Buzz
Apollo

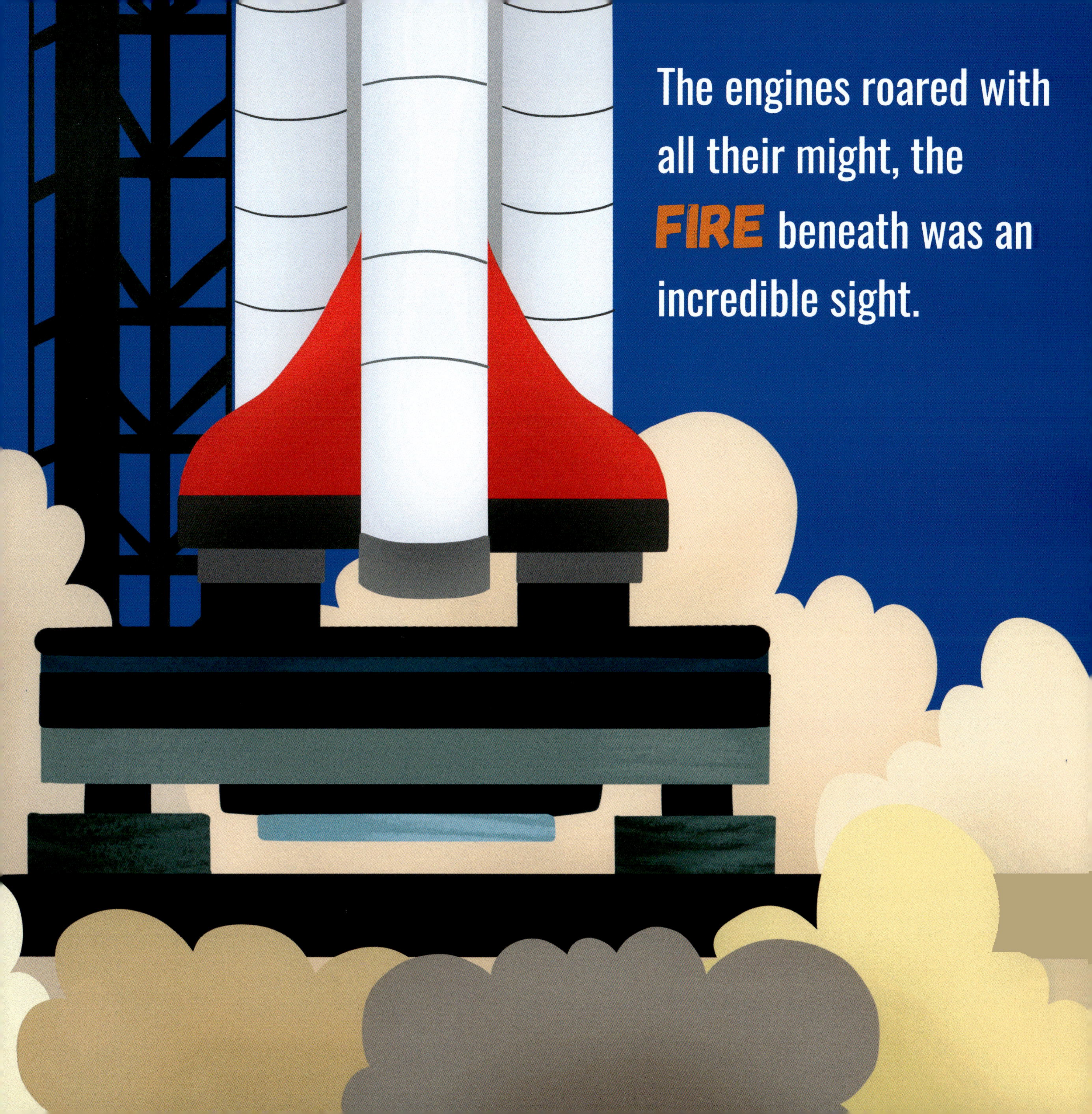

The engines roared with all their might, the **FIRE** beneath was an incredible sight.

5
4
3
2
1

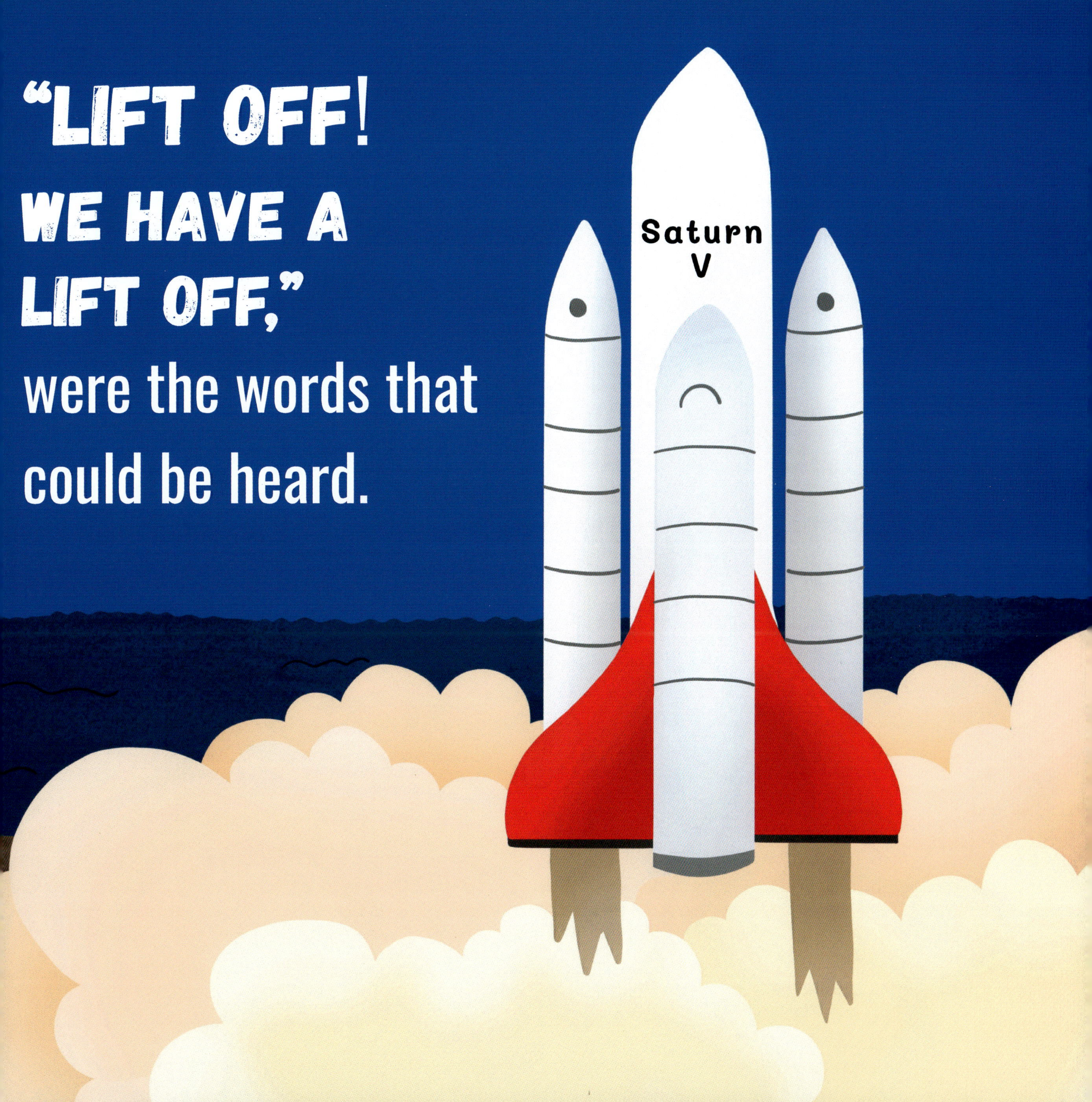
"LIFT OFF!
WE HAVE A
LIFT OFF,"
were the words that
could be heard.
Saturn
V

I can't believe this is happening Buzz, this is absolutely absurd
Neil
Neil
Apollo
Buzz
Buzz
Apollo

The **ROCKET** launched high into the clear blue sky.

"Hooray" they shouted, "I always knew we'd be able to **FLY**."

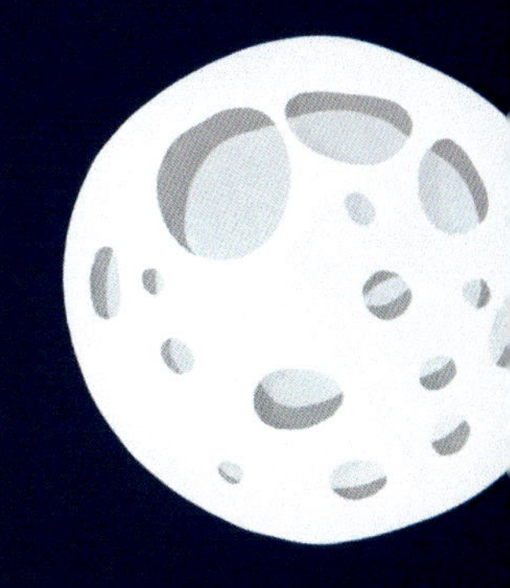

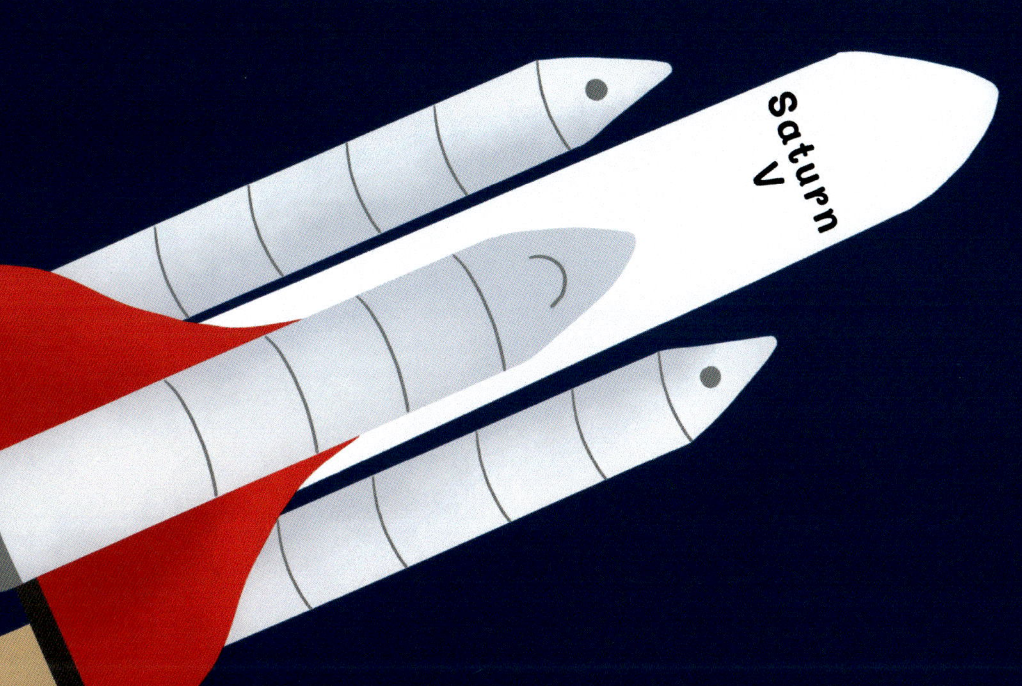

They made their way towards the Moon, but not so **FAST**.

Around the Earth they went, they needed a **BLAST**!

4 days went by, until they landed on the Moon. They landed with a **BOOM**, but not a moment too soon.

Neil stepped down the ladder, anxious to see what he might find, stating **"ONE SMALL STEP FOR MAN, ONE GIANT LEAP FOR MANKIND!"**

He bounced, hopped and jumped, shouting "**WOW**! **THIS IS REALLY COOL**!"

That's because there was no gravity at all!

He opened his sample bag, that was a must, one reason for being there was to collect some **MOONDUST**.

The cheers from Buzz could be heard very loudly,
as Neil staked his flag on the surface of the Moon proudly.

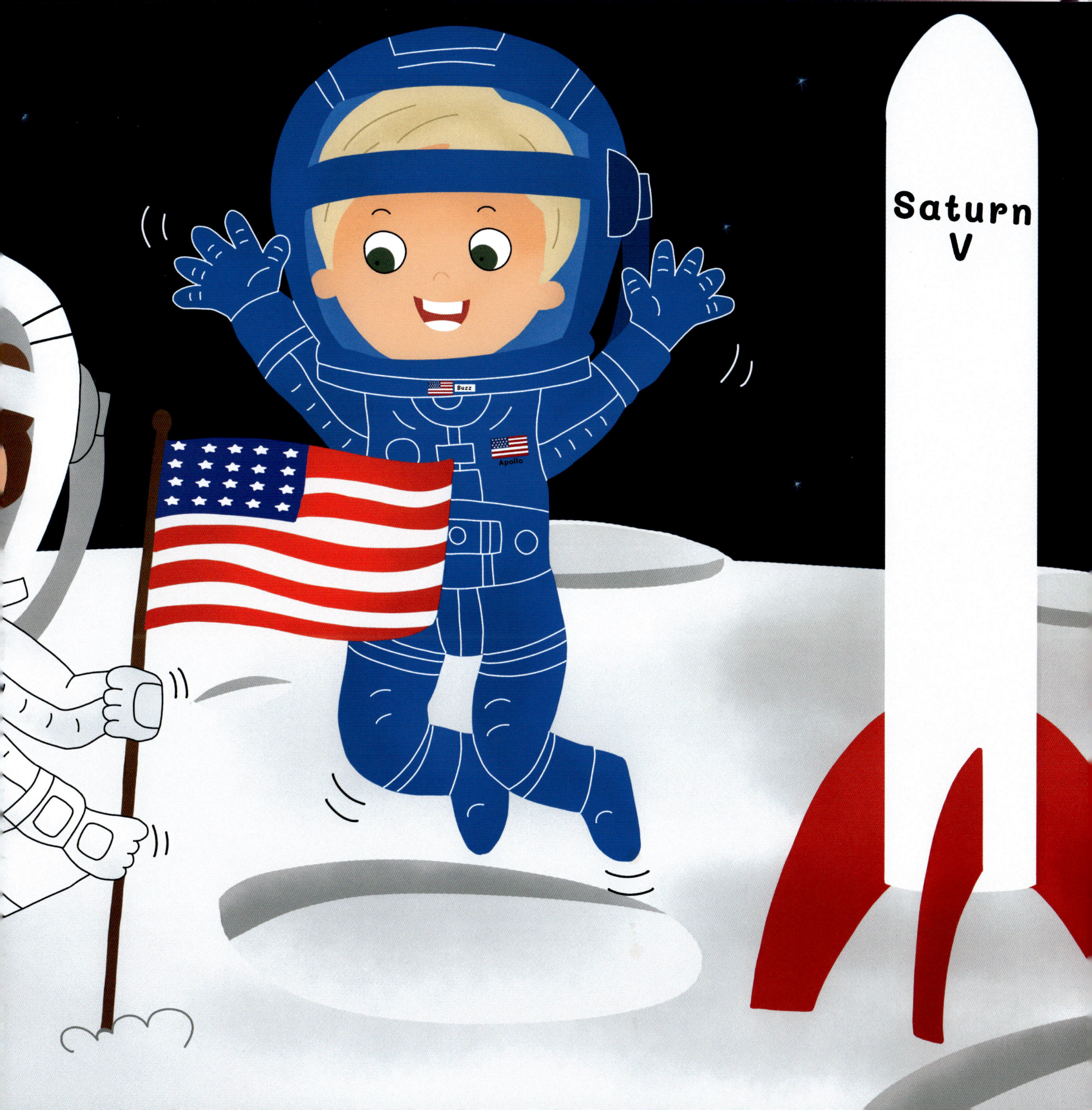
Saturn V
Buzz
Apollo

Two hours they stayed before heading back home, they were so happy to have been, where no other man had **FLOWN**.

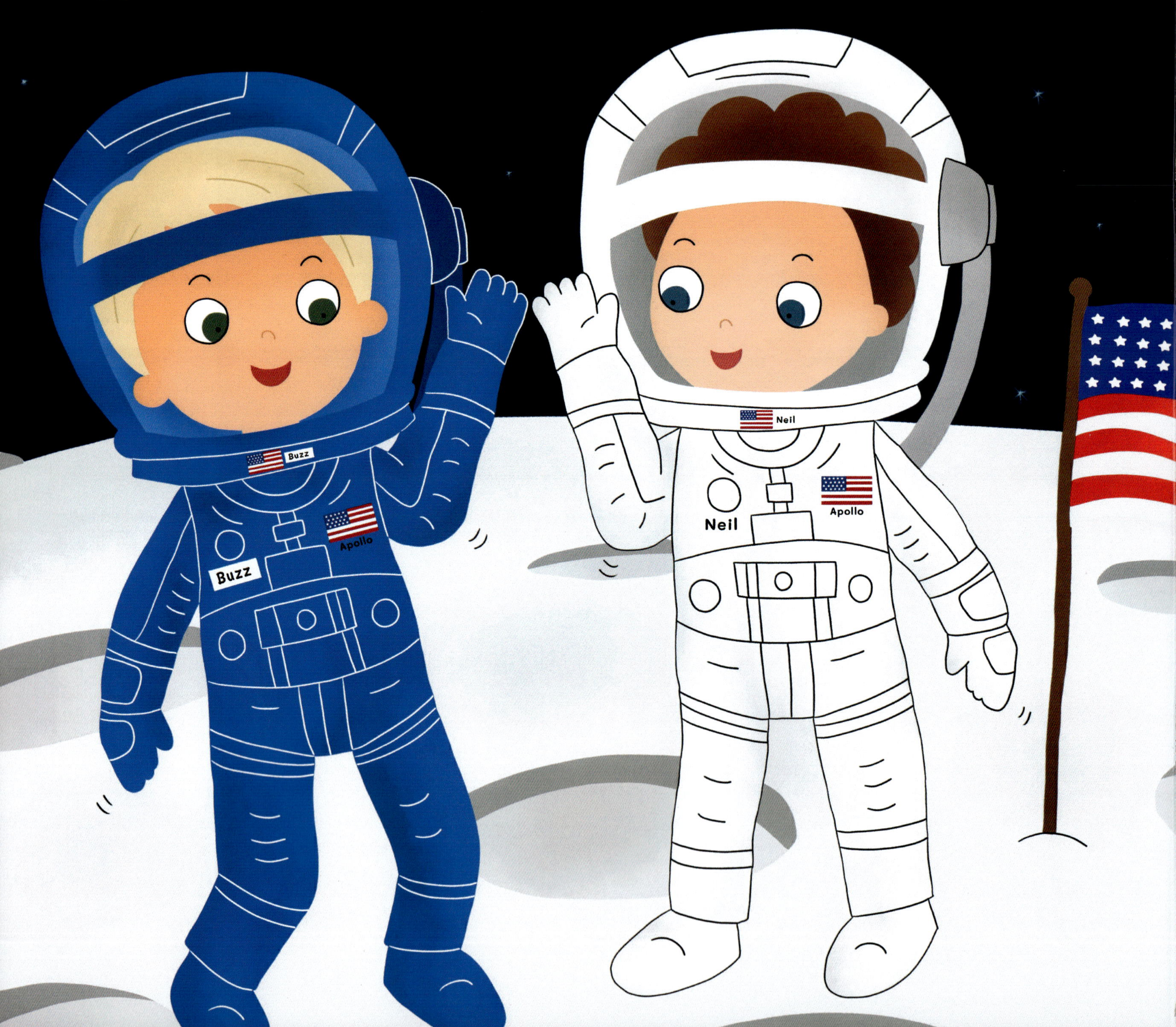

A little boy with a dream, to be the first person to walk on the Moon, came parachuting back to Earth safely, **WHISPERING**

“I HOPE TO
SEE YOU
AGAIN SOON,